COME TO MY VILLAGE

by Henriette Groot

Illustrated by Ardella Swanberg

Groot, Henriette, Author
Swanberg, Ardella, Illustrator
   Come to My Village

ISBN 978-0-9828492-5-5

1. Journal - Autobiography
2. Southeast Asia History
3. Sailing

Cover Illustration: Ardella Swanberg
Cover Design: Devin Henry
Technical Support: Devin Henry

Printed by Lightning Source, USA, UK and Australia.

Table of Contents

Chapter One:
An Invitation

We saw the light flashes while passing the village. A signal? We looked at each other. Should we go over and see what they wanted? But we had been flagged down before in the Solomon Islands, flagged down literally, by an old fellow dressed in flour sacks, madly waving a little white flag on a pole; and when we had gone ashore the poverty in that village had been so overwhelming we fled. Much later we learned from other yachts that the sack-cloth guy was well known, that this was his standard uniform and he tried to stop all passing boats. This time we sailed on to the next anchorage where we could see several boats already at anchor.

We put the anchor down and immediately local people in canoes arrived, wanting to talk, wanting to trade. We dealt with them rather quickly because we wanted to have lunch. It was after lunch that our friend-to-be arrived. He had a small boy with him in his canoe, one of his sons we learned later. He came alongside and slipped aboard easily to sit on the rail. He carried himself with such natural dignity that this did not even evoke our usual "You should ask for permission before coming aboard". He said his name was Manah Nendi and gave us both a firm handshake.

He was a slight, rather intense young man. His hair was shorter and of a softer texture than the usually so luxuriant mop of the Solomon islander. A.C. started to make small talk, his usual way of breaking the ice, but Manah had other things on his mind. Rather abruptly he says, "Come back to my village with me." How nice, we're being invited! But... what did he mean "come back"? Where is his village? Manah says his village is Honamusu, the one we just by-passed! Manah refers to himself as "the 'Acting Chief,' until the old Chief dies."

"Was that you, signalling us back there?"

"Yes."

Then both sides start to explain: we, a little sheepishly, that we hadn't been sure what the signal meant, and he, in half English-half Pidgin, that flashing a mirror is their way of inviting yachts to visit. He seems quite ready to forgive us for ignoring his signal (what if it had been an emergency?), but is rather indignant that yachts just pass by without giving each village a chance to show its carvings. But it isn't just the carvings, Manah says, "The people in the village want to meet the people on the yachts."

Manah hands us a flyer, a carbon copy, typed! The flyer reads verbatim:

Manah Nendi and his son welcoming yachts to their lagoon.

ALL YACHTSMEN VISITING MAROVO LAGOON:

The Peoples of Honamusu Village are interested in meeting Yachtsmen visiting the Lagoon. We would like to trade or sell our distinctive carvings, and all pieces are hand crafted. No two pieces exactly the same can be found.

Wooden objects:

a. War canoe

b. Prow or *Nuzu nuzu* is the most outstanding

c. the Custom carving Basket ware:

a. Famous Buka basket ware

b. Ordinary basket We also sell:

l. Sea shell

2. Tables mat

3. Custom cloth

Be sure to visit Honamusu Village. "ALL ARE WELCOME"

See Manah Nendi : a. the Acting Chief

b. Chairman of the Board, for the carving

Ando Nendi: a. Hand Crafted Director

Address: Honamusu, c/o Postal Agency Marovo Lagoon,

Via Honiara, Solomon Isl. pa

We are quite impressed by all this modern advertising and tell him so. Manah relaxes a bit. When he smiles, with his nice white teeth, he is really rather a pleasant young man. He repeats his entreaty to come back with him to his village. We tell him we had planned first to go to one of the smaller uninhabited islets to swim and relax. He won't have any of that! This is the *very* thing discussed in council meeting! ...that the yachts don't seem to understand that they should go to the villages *first*. (Ah, the chiefs meet in council, do they?) Then he comes up with, "We don't have tourists here. The yachts are our tourists." We acknowledge how nicely that concept puts us under a certain obligation and he is pleased at our understanding.

Having heard a few rumors about these chiefs planning to try to regulate yachts, however, we have a few questions of our own. Are they saying that we are *prohibited* from going to the outer anchorages, the one-palm tree islets which so appeal to the Robinson Crusoe in us? No, that is not quite the case. But the villagers would like to first meet these people who visit their property, and to be sure that they do not just help themselves to the fish and the shells and even the coconuts. Again we have to agree with him, for we have seen before how hard-pressed the limited resources of the lagoons and reefs are by the continual harvesting of local people, while we also know that some of our fellow yachtsmen don't seem to realize that everything on land or in the water belongs to someone. Every coconut tree is known and owned. And there is no freedom of the seas in the lagoon!

By now we are captivated. We check with each other with a glance, then say, "Yes, we will come to your village." Right away he wants to show us how to get there. He turns out to be quite familiar with the chart, but curiously shows us how to get there from the position we were at when he first signalled us! So we have to double-check to make sure the approach is clear from our present anchorage.

Then he starts to push, "When will you come?" We're not quite willing to commit ourselves. For a moment his face shows, what? ...anger? ...frustration? I ask whether he is planning to go on a trip or perhaps isn't home on certain days.

He calms down, "No, I'll be there."

We ask him to sign our guest log, which he does in a firm hand, adding, "Be sure to visiting Honamusu. All welcome." (Doesn't pass up an opportunity, does he?)

Then he shows us a sample of the carving. Out of his airline satchel, wrapped in cloth, comes a magnificent black ebony eagle! It's lines almost arrogant, well balanced on out-stretched talons and tail. Beautiful detail in the upswept wings. Later on I ask for a second look at it, I am tempted to try to buy it in accordance with our dictum "Buy it when you see it." (A dictum developed after many shopping trips to just one more obscure Chinese store while the first store sells the item I really wanted.) I tell Manah that I'm interested in the Eagle. He goes into a long involved explanation about "kastom" carvings. (Custom, meaning tradition or traditional is a key word in these islands.) He tells us the myth the eagle carving is based on. Unfortunately he is harder to understand while on this subject, the custom story seems to call for more Pidgin words than we are familiar with.

He tells us he has organized a show-room in the village for the carvings, so people won't have to come out to the yachts to sell their wares. I tell him I like that idea very much because having visitors to the boat at all times of the day is very tiring. Yes, that's why he tells his people not to keep bothering the yachts. He also tells them not to take anything belonging to a yacht; his people are "good people, don't steal." We are surprised at his even bringing this up and assure him that we have not had any problems whatsoever with theft in the Solomons.

He plans to send the advertising flyer to the Yacht Club in Honiara for posting. When I suggest that perhaps it should mention the showroom for carvings he asks me to write that for him so he can type it later. I decide to think it over and give him my suggestions for alterations when we visit the village.

He asks, "What do you have to trade?" (How many times were we to hear that question all through Marovo Lagoon!)

"Some old clothing and other stuff we don't need anymore."

"Do you have magazines? They are good to give ideas for carvings," he explains.

"Yes."

"Can I see?" We show him a Reader's Digest we'd saved in case we ran across someone trying to learn English. Manah lets us know that this would be a nice gift for him, the Acting Chief.

"Okay, when we get to the village." But he's determined to have his gift now and we relent. He picks up the binoculars and looks through them. (Some earlier visitors did not know how, but he does!)

"Do you have a second one?"

"No!"

Finally we break it up by telling him that we need to go ashore to shop. He takes off for some of the other boats and we put on our shore-going clothes, in my case a skirt instead of shorts. A.C. says, "That young man must have an MBA in marketing from Harvard, the only mistake he made was in getting too pushy about when we are to come to the village! And I bet a Yank helped him with that write-up, it's beautiful! But I think only the American boats will really respond to that, not the Aussies and Kiwis."

On our way to the beach we pass an Australian boat from which Manah is just leaving. So soon? We chat a bit with them and sure enough! To them Manah just came on too strong. They thought him too pushy altogether. They tried to buy the Eagle but he wouldn't sell it. Also, he demanded to sign their guest log! Had Manah used up all his tact with us or was our perception of his behavior just that different from theirs?

I discover I had forgotten my hat without which I can't stand the tropical sun, so we go back for it. When our dinghy finally is heading for the shore again we hear a sudden voice, "Oh, you forgot your hat?"

Manah's canoe reappears from behind the boat. What is he doing? Is his visit to the third boat already finished too? Now both our dinghy and his canoe are headed in the same direction. I suddenly wonder whether part of his pushiness was that he had hoped for a tow back home, rather than having to paddle all the way.

I call out, "Will it take you long to get back?"

He replies "No", but I suspect he is putting a brave face on it.

The next morning after breakfast we agree that as soon as we fill the water tanks we will head for Honamusu. Somehow that seems to be the next thing to do. Never in our five years of cruising all over the South Pacific had we ever had so compelling an invitation.

Chapter Two:
Visiting Honamusu Village

The weather is threatening and the overcast makes it difficult to see the reefs. But the really shallow patches are still distinct and our fathometer is very reliable, so we carry on.

An hour and a half later we drop anchor off the peninsula on which the village is located. A canoe with two kids comes out and is already hovering around while we are still setting the anchor. (Haven't they heard of their Acting Chief's good ideas about not bothering the yachts?)

They try to come alongside, but A.C. warns them off, "Not until we have finished anchoring." They look confused, as if they don't comprehend, so I use hand gestures to shoo them off. When we are quite sure the anchor is down to stay I finally look at them and say "Hello." The boy in back of the canoe is clearly the one in charge. He responds with a bright "hello." (So they do know some English?) The other one with the bright yellow hair, which quite a few Melanesians have, acts as though he wants to blend into the background. They look about ten years old.

"What is your name?"

"Derek," replies the leader.

I say my name, then ask the other one, "And your name?"

He says something I don't quite understand, so I ask, "A custom name?"

"Yes."

I tell them we're going to have lunch now and will come ashore afterwards. They either don't understand or are reluctant to leave, so I have to reinforce it with, "So goodbye for now, see you later."

Then, from below, fixing lunch, I hear A.C. talking to someone. A man has come out in his canoe. While A.C. tries to explain again that we don't want visitors right now, this fellow has his own message to get across, "Manah, the chief, is not here. He is in the bush working on a new canoe. Will you wait until tonight when Manah comes back?"

I ask, "Does that mean they don't want us to come ashore?"

But no, that is not the intent of the message.

After lunch and a siesta of dozing over a book we head for shore in the dinghy. Derek and friend are scooting about in their canoe, watching our every move. We call out, "Hello!" By the time we land Derek is also ashore, standing there with a long dangerous-looking bush knife, looking like a sentinel. We admire the knife. We comment to one another how all the island kids seem to be trusted with sharp knives; we've even seen the very young with them.

We ask, just for the form, "To the village, this way?"

"Yes," Derek takes off with us in single-file behind him.

The path winds along the shore. Many orchid-like flowers in the bush. Houses are scattered on both sides of the path. The ones on the lagoon side extend out over the water. A very new thatch house has a lock on the door. Next to it a two-story one on piles. Then a boat-house with some canoes; we recognize Manah's canoe of yesterday by its name. Then a timber house, and a house in ruins. Some children appear and fall in behind us. A young man is sitting under a thatch awning, carving. He is not very interested in making conversation. Next we come upon two older men under a bush, carving combs.

A.C. makes a joke, "How come they need combs?" They're almost bald and A.C. rubs his head to show how sparse his own hair is on top. Everybody laughs.

We move on. Neat plantings appear along the path, which is covered with clean coral gravel. Then we come to the Bakery! We know it's the Bakery, because it has a little flag that says "The Bakery." The flag can be raised by means of a halyard, but it is in the down position and the door is locked. Do they raise the flag when the bread is done? We pass a spacious church. Then more people appear, women weaving baskets, and also some men. They're friendly but we run out of conversation soon, so we push on. More houses, a copra-drying shack and another boathouse with a large canoe showing a gaping crack. We speculate that one really could do a job here fixing canoes with modern epoxy products, so many of the wooden canoes have holes.

We run out of village. What to do now? We've hardly talked with the villagers, between their shyness and our not wanting to intrude we just sort of breezed through! We decide we'd best wait for Manah's return, at least we feel we know him. Meanwhile we are having a nice walk, though we've lost our charming escort of children. We come into a coconut plantation, "Looks like they harvest them, there are very few nuts left on the trees." Suddenly we hear voices behind us. With much shouting and laughing the kids catch up to us. There are big ones, little ones, boys, girls, dressed and nude. The leader, of course, is Derek.

Curious about the many coconuts on the ground with holes in them, I ask, "Did coconut crabs do this?"

"No, a purt, a red purt," Derek and another boy, also an English-speaker, explain. I look puzzled. They point at the treetops, and then I see and hear them, bright red parrots flying from tree to tree, squawking. That's right, we have heard somewhere about plans for killing parrots and cockatoes because of the damage they do to the coconuts. Derek runs to the head of the parade and the use for the sling-shot I've seen around his neck becomes apparent. He shoots a pebble at the parrots. They fly off, sqawking loudly.

Parrots, cockatoes and children in the coconut trees.

A side-path leading back to the lagoon opens up. We want to try it; can't be away from the water too long! A.C. is leading and when he gets to the water's edge he keeps walking on, right into the water. The children and I stop at the water's edge. He takes a few more steps, looks back, asks, "Aren't you coming with me?"

He has to repeat his little joke and then everybody laughs.

The kids and I check out the flotsam and jetsam on the little beach: an old Adida bag and another plastic bag. How far did these envoys of "civilization" travel? For a moment I consider picking them up to put them into the special bag we keep aboard the *Barones* for plastic refuse, which gets dumped when we get back to civilization, but then my Sierra Club conscience deserts me. We turn back.

Now the order of progression has changed and I am last. A tiny little girl looks back to see whether I am coming. How nice, I feel part of the group! When we get back to the fork in the path, A.C. shows me a nut he has found.

"Could this be a *nali* nut?" We haven't seen these anywhere but in the Solomons, but they're delicious! *Nali* nuts taste like a cross between an almond and fresh heart of palm. I show it to Derek who says no, it isn't *nali*. I ask him to show me a *nali* tree if they have them here. Derek and I seem to be the communication link.

On we go. Derek plunks away at some more parrots which the kids busily point out to him. We pass an isolated thatch hut which seems to be a drying shed for copra.

Derek says, "Belong Manah." I wonder at that. I had thought it was all community property.

By now we've come almost full circle around the peninsula. Another choice point presents itself. A.C. and the little nudist who has been walking point march off to the left, but Derek suggests, "Go this way." I repeat this to A.C. who turns back. The little nudist, however, keeps heading deeper into the bush. After a lot of yelling from the other kids, however, he finally turns around to come with us.

The plantation here, although rather overgrown, shows signs of work. Coconuts lie sorted into piles, sprouting nuts in one pile, empty shells in another. Derek is getting busier and busier. He shows me a small nut, "*nali!*" He pounds it open and gives it to me. I thank him. He also is going after more parrots, which indeed are over-abundant.

I worry about a stray pebble hitting one of the kids, but just when one of the kids is standing too close to the target area, all the others yell at him. The kids, when pointing out birds to Derek seem to be playing on his name, it sounds like:

"Derek, Dereki, Deriketti."

Just as I think he is going to be too busy to show me what a *nali* tree looks like, he points, "*Nali* tree!" He goes off into some very dense bush. The other English-speaking boy comes up to me and points too, "*Nali!*" Ah! I had been looking at the wrong tree. The *nali* is the one with the peeling reddish bark.

We climb a slight rise. On top is a football field! The kids point out more *nali* trees and the village below. I marvel at the energy of the children after our long walk, the smallest ones look like they're under two.

When we get back to the village we discuss whether we should invite the children out to the boat to play them some tapes. But our little group has already dispersed and Derek himself has disappeared. As we row back toward *Barones*, a canoe rounds the point. Derek and his side-kick! Our every move is being anticipated! Too bad that the other kids could not join us, but perhaps they don't all have the use of a canoe.

I ask Derek, "You come boat now and we play some music?" They smile and follow.

At the boat they need another invitation to come aboard. They don't have a line to tie the canoe. Side-kick holds up one of our lines and looks at me questioningly. I don't see anything on the canoe to tie on to, so he holds the canoe with one foot. I put on a cassette of Fijian music. They like it and smile. Sidekick by now has tied the canoe with one of our lines, there was a small nail on the bow after all. I smile approvingly at him. Another boy, a little older, arrives. The three kids and I make a tour of the boat. They ask where we're from. I show them the American flag astern, and then their own flag, the courtesy flag, at the spreaders, which I made myself! They recognize their own flag. I practice the name of Derek's side-kick, a sound between "Pada" and "Panda." I can't quite get it right. We laugh about that, but I am worried that the boy might think the laughter is directed at his nice custom name, so I say, "Stupid of me."

I ask them whether they go to school. Yes, they do. I don't quite catch where, not in the village, it seems, anyway. Today is a holiday, that's why they're not in school. The new boy is named John.

Then I recognize the fine features, "You are Manah's son?"

"Yes."

A little doubtfully I ask, "But was it you who came out to the boat with your father yesterday?"

In chorus they reply, "No, that was ---" I didn't catch the name, but I suppose the whole village knows who goes where and when!

I ask the boys to sign our guest log. Only John is up to that, with a very serious mien he writes, "John Manah." The other two run to the foredeck, away from this challenge. I write their name for them, and they come back to inspect. Why can't they write? They go to school and their English is really quite passable.

John leaves. A.C. is below in his radio corner and I settle down with a book. Derek and Pada seem quite content to just look around the boat without disturbing anything. Occasionally I get up to change the cassette. They seem to like island music best: Fiji, Samoa and Tonga. "Custom" music from Vanuatu does not go over quite so well.

When I put some on, they call out, "PNG!" (Papua New Guinea)

So I explain, "Old time music, from Vanuatu."

They look down their noses at Helen Reddy, the next one.

A canoe with a handsome grey-haired chap comes alongside. He seems shy and his English is not very good, but he has a very appealing smile, so I enjoy chatting with him. After asking where we're from he tells me he is Manah's brother, actually his ELDER brother. (Aha, do they follow the good Polynesian system of picking the most capable fellow for chief then, rather than just following seniority? This one certainly does not have Manah's drive.) He declines my invitation to come aboard because he's on his way to go fishing.

Off the point we see some Japanese fishing boats, slowly trawling for bait. He points them out to me.

"Are they in your part of the lagoon?" I ask.

"Yes"

"And do they pay twenty-eight dollars a night?" We'd heard about Japanese trawlers combing the lagoons for bait.

"Yes."

A canoe is approaching from the inner bay. "That's my father." (So the old chief is not ailing? ...as we had imagined?) He explains the ex-chief has been over at the next peninsula, helping a friend build a house.

"There are no people there," in fact the inland area is completely uninhabited.

"He likes to go there." Perhaps for that very reason? Apparently here, as in other South Sea islands, the missionaries arriving by boat settled on the shore, which drew the population to the shoreline. Missionaries also effected the nuzu nuzu, the decorative prow on the canoes: previously a human skull, but now the carved likeness of a dove.

Elder Brother has to go now. He paddles towards the canoe with the two old gentlemen and I distinctly hear the word "America." The two old-timers, grey-haired and balding, come over to visit. They have some English and explain that they have been building a house. By this time my husband has come out of his radio corner down below and there is general talk about WW II in the Solomons. Everyone remembers the Americans from those days. They ask A.C. whether he was here during the war. No, he was too young, but he was in the Navy, stationed in Hawaii, at the end of the war. We tell them about the 40th Anniversary of Guadalcanal - celebrations which we witnessed in Honiara, just a few weeks earlier.

Another canoe arrives with a message, "The people are ready for you to see the carvings."

"Okay, everybody off the boat for now." We put on our shore-going clothes and are ready to go again.

Chapter Three:
Carvings, Trades & Gifts

When we enter the village there is no one to be seen.

"But where do we go?" I fuss.

"They'll show us, no doubt." A.C. is always less worried about things.

Again we pass the two old fellows. They're no longer working on their combs, now they are sanding walking sticks. They point further down the path. And there, at the water's edge, the whole village is assembled! The handicraft work is neatly arranged on a covered porch, each item with price tag attached. There are many carvings in various stages of completion: ebony porpoises, kerosene wood turtles, sharks, fishes and several "Spirit of the Solomons" carvings (usually a gnarled branch or root from which a profusion of assorted sea-creatures is brought out of the turn of the wood), also some fine straw baskets and purses. We look at all these articles, with the whole village watching us. Neither of us finds anything particularly to our liking, but how do we get out of this?

To gain time I show Manah's advertising flyer to the man who came to fetch us to the exhibit. As I suspect, he is the "Hand Crafted" Director. He looks at the page as though he has never seen it. Can he read? I tell him we would like to buy some bread. We all go to the Bakery, which has to be unlocked first. The delicious smell inside spells fresh bread!

Handicraft Director says, "Two cakes for ten cents."

"Can we have six?" He discusses this with some of the other people, then brings out another carton with smaller rolls explaining that these are the "cakes" that are two for ten. We don't have exact change, so they have to pull the jar with change from its hiding place above the inner door.

That transaction completed we return to the show room. We handle some of the objects again. Some new items have arrived in the meantime, a nice large *Buka* basket amongst others. I again rue the smallness of our boat which restricts the size of souvenirs we can collect. I decide to buy a small change purse marked $4.50 just to buy something, but tell the Director that I'd like to trade rather than pay cash.

He looks doubtful, "Belong another woman."

"Would you ask her?"

"She not here." Stalemate. (They *did* mention trading on the flyer, didn't they?)

A.C. wants one of the dolphins priced at one dollar fifty. Will they trade for that one? It turns out to be one of the Director's own carvings, but he does not want to trade.

"I have a wife and children. I need money." A.C. pays him.

I ask for Manah's Eagle. He says it's in Manah's house. Then he points, "The woman is here," apparently the purse lady. I look at him expecting his help in the negotiations, but he doesn't make a move, so I go over to her. She agrees to trade and accepts my invitation to come to the boat tomorrow morning to pick something from our trade bag. Retired Chief is standing nearby in the crowd and says, "My daughter."

I take it he is referring to the purse lady. He also points out her husband and his own wife, a lady with an impressively large hat. The whole village must be one big family.

I say, "You have a nice family, nice village." Now he gets into the sales act, picks up a straw hat and asks whether I'd like it.

"Thank you, I have plenty hats."

Back at the showroom A.C. is still talking to the Director. He wants a kerosene wood thresher shark marked $4.50, but only if he can trade. The Director is quizzing him about what we have to trade. He asks for cassettes! A.C. tells him too to come out to the boat tomorrow.

Then suddenly Manah is there. But he doesn't come over to us, he now seems as shy as the other villagers. I go to him to ask about the Eagle. He says he does not want to sell it. Since it seems to be better quality than other things in the show room I wonder whether they keep it as a model attraction. So I say I understand and pull out the advertising hand-out to show him my revisions. But he does not want to talk now. (Too much of an audience?)

"I will come to the boat this evening, at six o'clock."

Nuzu nuzu, decorative carving for the prow of a canoe.

After that we don't really know what to do with ourselves anymore and decide to head back to the boat. At one of the last houses of the village we see the family having dinner inside, sitting on mats on the ground. We call out a "hello." The man comes out to talk, but we've run out of small talk, so we make our excuses. We get back to the boat at a quarter past six.

"But didn't Manah say he was coming over at six?"

"Yes. Oh well...."

Just as we sit down for dinner a canoe arrives with a bump against the hull. That always irritates me, and in the middle of dinner no less... So I don't budge. A.C. goes up into the cockpit to tell them we're just having dinner. It's Manah and the Director, wanting to trade for the thresher shark. A.C. asks, "Can you come back tomorrow?"

The reply is long and involved, something to the effect that Younger Brother, also known as the Hand Crafted Director, has to go somewhere tomorrow. So A.C. lets them come aboard . I stay below, eating my dinner, trying to ignore the whole thing. However, pretty soon I'm called into service too, I'm asked to put on the two cassettes we have to trade, an Elvis and a Glen Campbell. The Director wants to hear them both. Then he wants them both. As they had cost two or three dollars on sale in Brisbane that was a pretty fair trade.

Then they want to see what else we have to trade. (What for? We don't want anything else!) Manah asks for 22 bullets. A.C. says, "No, that would be illegal." They talk him into digging out the trade bag and start pawing through it. I hear Manah saying, "This is all old, next time bring new things." A.C. explains that we hadn't planned on doing all this trading, these are just things we've declared surplus in order to have anything at all to trade. By that time I have reached the boiling point and snap at A.C., "Do you have to do all this in the middle of dinner?" He lets me know his displeasure at my interference, but soon after I hear him say, "R. is upset, she would like to have dinner in peace." (Thank you, dear!) That gets them moving, until Manah suddenly stops, "But what about the Eagle?"

A.C. is firm, "Tomorrow, please."

Just as he sits back down we hear another canoe arrive. He goes back up. I hear someone saying that the fish wouldn't bite tonight. A.C. starts to give him the "we-are-having-dinner,-can-you-come-back-tomorrow" routine when the man offers him a pineapple.

A.C. calls down, "Do you want to buy a pineapple?"

The other voice, "No, not buy, *GIFT!*"

By now I realize it's Elder Brother, so I go topside too. Is it him? It's very dark and his gray hair is covered with a tattered pandanu hat. I thank him for the nice gift. We chat for a moment about the fish which must be sleeping instead of allowing themselves to get caught, then he leaves and finally we are able to finish dinner.

Chapter Four:
Breakfast, Bargaining & Bread

Next morning while preparing breakfast I look out of the porthole and see Manah approaching. I sort of flinch and move out of his line of sight. I'm not quite awake, not even dressed yet. A.C. goes up to receive him. I don't feel like getting involved yet and fuss with breakfast. However, I'm enticed out of my mood: Manah has brought us some breakfast! Still hot from the oven, too! We offer a cup of tea but he prefers Milo.

We try out his food, "Very good!"

He beams, "My wife made it. This morning I put it in the oven which still was hot."

The food is quite tasty. There is some tapioca pudding like no tapioca I ever had before with *nali* nuts in it, and there is a *masi masi* which looks like a lasagna of cooked cabbage, potato and *nali*. Both are firm and easy to cut, also easy to pick up and eat with the fingers. As appetizing as any local food we've eaten.

Then a flood of visitors overwhelms us. The Handicraft Director brings Sister-who-made-my-purse plus some children. (What happened to the trip he was going on?) The old Friend of the Retired Chief arrives, and Derek and Pada in their canoe. I almost don't recognize my friend Derek for he is quite dressed up today, shirt and all. I am kept busy below making cups of Milo for everyone. A.C. is in the cockpit entertaining the adults,

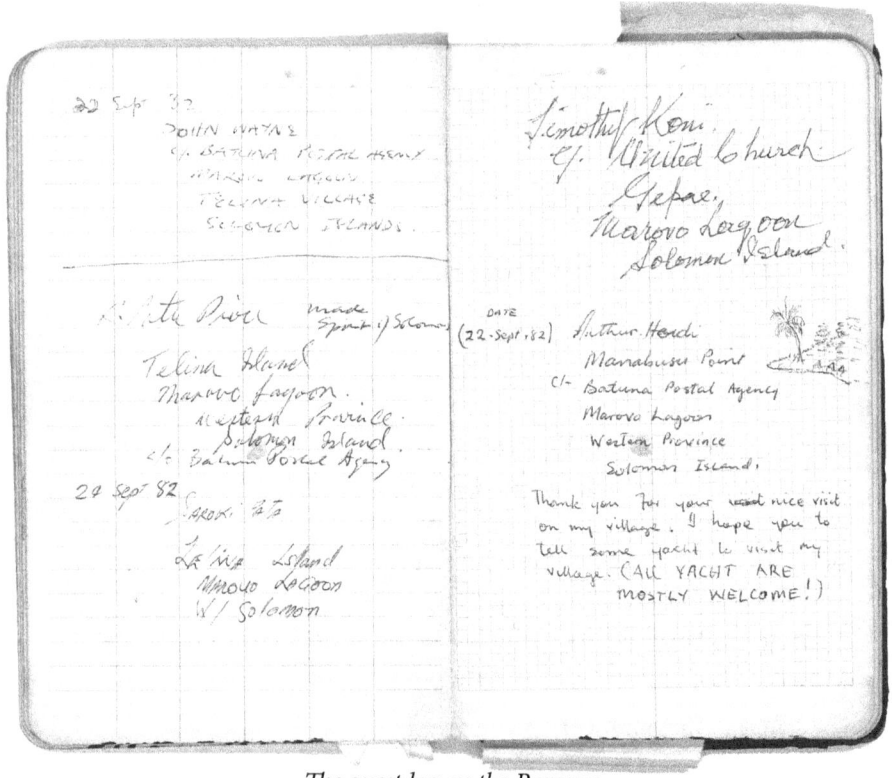

The guest log on the Barones.

while the kids are running around on deck and jumping in and out of canoes. Everyone has to sign the guest log. Manah is quite determined that they all perform this ritual. The Director, true to his metier, draws a picture in the log as well, recognizably Honamusu on its peninsula. I see Manah playing with the friendly pretty girl of yesterday. I wonder if she is his daughter. Elder Brother arrives too and is persuaded to join us for a Milo. I praise the delicious pineapple he brought yesterday.

Sister-who-made-my-purse is shy like most Melanesian village women. She doesn't take part in the general conversation. I decide to call her below for our trading session. She takes a long time, carefully checking each item in the bag. She is interested in some shorts for her husband, ignoring a woman's blouse.

I comment, "Your husband is lucky, you think of him first."

She again looks at the one sheet, fingering a small hole in it. She decides she wants the sheet as well as the shorts. I tell her that's a little much, but she can have either one plus one of the smaller items. She picks the sheet and a piece of bright flowered "calico" from Tahiti.

I show her what I am cooking in the pressure cooker and have her taste a piece of banana bread. She goes back up to the cockpit and shares the banana bread with some of the others, so now I had better give everybody some. Thinly sliced there is just enough to go around.

They like it, "Sweet!" And here I had forgotten to put some sugar in!

Retired Chief's Friend has a purpose to his visit. He produces a hunting license, paid-up and all! It's in his name and cost him $10 a year. He really would like some bullets, for shooting pigs in the mountains, crocodiles in the creeks (yes, they have crocodiles!), and, last but not least, to shoot those "purts" that steal the coconuts. The license persuades A.C. to give him some bullets, which makes everybody very happy indeed. We feel it really is a gift for the whole village.

They tell us they visited the Japanese trawler last night. It was a busy night for visiting, it seems! So this constant patrolling of their territory is how they collect from all the visitors!

A.C. asks me, "What about the Eagle?"

"Does he want to sell it?" I ask.

"He brought it, in his satchel," he replies.

So I ask Manah about the Eagle. He decides to come below, too, for this transaction. He wants thirty dollars cash for a trip to Honiara and the rest in trade. I ask whether he really wants to sell it now. Yes, he has made up his mind. Finally!

Manah's eagle carving.

"How long would it take to make another Eagle?"

"About four days."

Then I feel less bad about taking his treasure. I dig out the cash box and see we are almost out of cash. It will be a long while before we can get to another bank for there are none here in Marovo Lagoon, but I pay him the thirty dollars anyway. For the trading part I pull out the trade goods bag.

He looks down his nose at that, "I saw that last night."

He fingers the pillow behind him which serves as a stuff-bag for my clothes.

"I like this," he says.

"But that's mine!" I exclaim almost indignantly. (It was a going-away gift from my mother.)

"You can get another."

I offer to pay more cash. He laughs that off. He's probably is having too much fun coveting everything on the boat! He peers into the dark recesses of the quarterberths and I feel positively threatened. What will he come up with next? I show the knives again, which we had thought would be popular as trade items. He's not interested, but Elder Brother, watching from the cockpit, is!

Manah keeps asking, "But don't you have anything else to trade?" And then he comes out with it. Sometimes yachts claim they have nothing else, and then in the next village they pull out a whole new bag of goodies! (So he is suspecting us of holding out on him?)

Again I reiterate, "We didn't come to your country to trade, we came to visit."

Trading we do only incidentally, when people offer us carvings and ask to trade. (Actually, we sometimes offer to trade when the cashbox is low.) Anyway, I assure him we don't have a bag with marvelous things hidden away. Being a small, 35-foot boat we only carry what we need ourselves. If we don't need something anymore then it ends up in the trade bag.

"Here is the skirt I wore yesterday, I've had it too long, any day now I will be ready to get rid of it. Do you want it?" That seems to get across, but he still is fingering my pillow-bag. "Is it waterproof?"

A.C. who laughingly had called down, "I am keeping out of this," now comes to my rescue. Perhaps Manah would like the extra foul weather jacket?

He tries on the bright yellow jacket and likes it, "It's different," he notes proudly. (Does he harbor a need to stand out from the crowd?) He decides he'll take it. Elder Brother says something to him and he adds, "And the knife for him." I feel he is carrying things a little far, but A.C. says, "Okay."

As I hand the knife to Elder Brother I make a fine point by saying, "Okay, a gift for you from us." (After all, we have had a different type of relationship with him, one of gift-giving, and the pineapple was truly delicious.)

Meanwhile the cockpit has cleared out a bit. Several canoe-loads had left. Elder Brother takes off too, to go fishing again. Manah seems firmly ensconced in his corner in the main cabin. He wants our address so we can write to each other. Perhaps he will send us a carving for Christmas. He pulls a notebook out of his satchel for me to write our address. Then he asks for my banana cake "receipt."

"Oh, the recipe," I reply.

Next he asks whether I have typing paper. Now I feel rather pressed and show it in my expression.

He hastily adds, "I want to buy."

"Okay," but how much would I charge? Or, just make it a gift anyway? I can't quite decide, so meanwhile I start writing out the recipe for him. I check whether they have baking powder. They do. My "2 T" and "1 t" has to be translated into tablespoons and teaspoons. I show him the size of spoons this refers to. Do they have raisins? He doesn't know raisins. I show him some and he takes one to taste.

"Sweet! Do they have in Honiara?"

I couldn't find any when I was shopping there, but they did have candied lemon peel which should be as good. I give him some lemon peel to taste. He says they have lemons.

"How do you make lemon peel?" I don't know but am intrigued by the question and enjoy his keenness to try new things.

"I suppose you would dry them, or would you first soak the peel in sugar water? You'd have to watch out you don't make alcohol by mistake!" We all laugh. Being Seventh Day Adventists they are all confirmed teetotalers.

While I'm still writing the recipe, he suddenly says, "Flies on the food; cover it."

And yes, there are flies. More than usual, because the breakfast dishes haven't been done. Who has time for dishes with all these visitors? I cover up the food, though a little choked up over his peremptory tone. (Is that how they speak to their women? More likely just due to his limited English.) I return to the recipe. Next I pull out some typing paper, still unable to decide about that charging business. (Fifty cents? But how ridiculous!) I tell him the banana bread should not be baked too fast. I can't quite visualize their type of oven. Is it an earth oven? (Most likely, since he had said the oven was still hot at breakfast time.) Is it uniformly hot or is there a cooler part?

Next he asks for a recipe for bread.

"But we enjoyed your rolls!"

Yes, they are good, but he also wants bread. A previous visiting yacht gave them all the ingredients for bread, but left without giving them the recipe.

He amends, "He forgot to give it and I forgot to ask for it."

Now I really have a chore in transcribing my bread recipe, for it is one for yachts, utilizing some salt water instead of salt in order to cut down on fresh water consumption. And it's for wheat flour. What kind of flour do they have?

"White."

Oh well, that probably should be alright. But, do they have yeast? Yes, they have. And do they know to use warm-but-not-too-hot water on the yeast? (Stop worrying, those rolls were fine!) Then, when I write "grease the pan" I wonder whether that is a meaningful statement to them. Suddenly I realize they probably don't even have a pan. I show him a loaf pan, explaining that this is also the kind of pan I use for the banana bread. No, they don't have anything like that.

"Any other kind of metal pan?"

"No," inevitably, now he wants my pan!

"I buy it."

But my recipe calls for two pans! Oh well, I probably could use a stainless bowl for the second loaf.

"Okay, one pan for you, one for me."

Now I still have to explain that my recipe was for two pans, so everything has to be halved. I'm still worried about how well my recipe communicates, and for a moment consider making some bread together, but that does not seem a good idea either. Once more I say I am not at all sure how well the recipe will work out, they may have to add flour if the dough is not right, they may have to experiment.

He reassures me that he realizes the dilemma, saying, "It's all in the hands."

I agree wholeheartedly. I notice we both have been illustrating by making kneading motions with our hands!

He adds, "People ask me about our cakes. I taught that man myself."

So Manah started the Bakery and taught his brother?

He says, "I will think of you two when I use that pan," which endears him to me all over again. To me also gifts are reminders of the people behind them.

Meanwhile A.C. has come below and is doing the dishes, his usual chore. He asks Manah whether he has to do dishes at home. Manah says sometimes, when his wife has worked all day. He even cooks at times.

Next we turn to the flyer inviting yachts to Honamusu. Manah copies my additions which mention the showroom ashore. By now I realize there is little point in claiming that canoes won't come out to the yachts as they obviously will, but at least this may take some of the pressure off.

Then I think of something else, "We should mention the Bakery, the yachts will want bread!"

"Okay, you write the English. I type. My English not so good." He adds he has two typewriters, one large and one portable, "about that size" and he points at my typewriter half-way down the quarterberth. Has this eagle-eyes missed anything?

He inquires, "What religion do you have?"

A.C. replies he has none but that he attended a lot of churches in his younger days.

Manah turns to me, "And you?"

I tell him I'm a Quaker. He has never heard of Quakers.

"Do they believe in God?" I take the easy way out and just say, "Yes," thus missing a good opportunity to tell what Quakers are all about: a belief in "that of God within each of us." Manah has no such reluctance and starts preaching the Seventh Day Adventist version of Christianity. We listen politely, non-committally, until I make the mistake of asking a question.

He starts to answer, then, "Do you have a Bible, I'll show you." Surprise! I pull one out of the bookcase. He starts reading some awful passage from Prophesies about "the mark of the Beast," apparently an important element in SDA theology. One of us suggests we move to the cockpit which serves to break up the sermon.

He has another item on his agenda. He pulls a news magazine from his inexhaustible satchel, opens it to an article about the Falklands war and wants A.C. to explain.

Who are the Falklands, "*Hemi* independent?" (*Hemi* is Pidgin for "he" or "they".)

And Argentina, "*Hemi* independent?" (We are reminded that independence is still fairly recent in these islands and a matter of great pride.) We take turns explaining that Argentina used to belong to Spain.

That he understands readily, "*belong*" is the most frequently used word in Pidgin. He wants to know who first came to the Falklands.

"Spain, but the first settlers were English!"

We all agree it's an awful mess. He points at a picture of one of the missiles, and again we agree it is terrible.

We ask Manah about his schooling. He went as far as the seventh grade, at an SDA school on another island. A high level of education for here!

I check into their naming system, "What do people call you?"

"Manah Nendi."

"Yes, I know, but what do your friends call you?"

"Manah."

He explains that Nendi is his father's name (the Retired Chief, presumably).

"Oh, that's why your son is John Manah. So his son would be *something* John?"

We tell him that Europeans had this system in the past, for example "John Jacobson" meant "John son of Jacob."

Chapter Five:
Sailing On

Finally we come to the question of when do we leave. Somehow all three of us (including Manah!) agree that today is the day. Something feels completed. Also, we feel squeezed dry, of information and of gifts. The reason Manah is willing to let us go may be that another yacht is approaching in the distance. He has been watching it. He borrows our mirror to signal them! He recommends we go to the next village. We are not committing ourselves, but he shows the way anyway. It is a "nice village," but at the village after that we have to watch out, for those people are "thieves." But please, we should not mention that to the next village (the nice one), for they are related of the thieves.

Elder Brother drops by again. This time he has been successful and A.C. admires the fish lying in the bottom of the canoe. Elder Brother holds one up to show me, saying nothing, but clearly offering it as a gift if I want it. I admire it duly and receive the fish. (Now when am I going to find time to clean and cook that? We have no refrigeration.)

A.C. goes to the foredeck to do some work on the anchor chain. Manah starts to pack his satchel and asks, "So how much?" I had almost forgotten our not-quite-completed negotiations over the typing paper. I am glad he asks, it makes me feel like being magnanimous, "They are gifts for you and the village."

The Barones sails on.

Another canoe arrives. I ask Manah to please tell them we are getting ready to leave. He does so, then states that he himself will stay until just before we go. Actually I had hoped he would take the hint, but oh well, he almost seems like a member of the crew by now. I may just surprise him and ask him to help me take down the awning! As I am picking stuff off the deck (how does a cruising yacht develop clutter so fast?) we somehow get to talking about mosquitoes. He says they don't have many here, then wants to know whether we have mosquito coils.

Defensively I say, "Yes, but we need them ourselves." (I am forever being bitten.)

"What, but you don't have mosquitoes on the water."

"Oh yes, we do!" He persists, really wanting some.

I get half-way mad, "Don't you like the gifts we've given you?"

He withdraws quickly, "Oh yes, I do!"

Just as I'm about to ask him to help with that awning he really does take off for the new yacht. Soon we see several canoes clustered around the boat as it anchors. Manah is first aboard! After our anchor is up, we go past them to say hello. Their flag is German. We call out, "Nice village, nice people."

As we head out of the anchorage a mirror starts to flash at us from the next village…

About the Author

Henriette Groot, author, sailor, psychologist and Quaker, started sailing in Holland, her native country. She completed a near-circumnavigation over seventeen years with her husband, Albert Carlisle Mayes (A.C.). Henriette is a clinical psychologist, with a PhD (1960) from UCLA. She became a Quaker in Australia during their world cruise. She is now retired, living in Los Osos, California with two cats, two llamas and a dog. She is active in her local Friends Meeting. As an activist, she is concerned about climate change, deterioration of democracy in the West, destructive impacts of Western "civilization" on other cultures, and the disastrous legacy of nuclear waste to untold future generations. Email: hplgroot@KCBX.net Ham call: KC6VYB

She and her husband, A.C., visited Honamusu Village, Marovo Lagoon in September 1982. They reached the Florida coast by 1991, then continued sailing the Americas until 1994. In 1995 A.C. was diagnosed with cancer, so they returned home with the boat to California by way of the I-10 Highway.

The photo to the right shows Henriette Groot (right) and Ardella Swanberg (left) on the *Barones.*

About the Illustrator

Ardella Swanberg, an artist and native of California, she studied art education at the University of Minnesota, married an engineer and spent the next 30 years following him to his jobs. She has traveled through most of the United States and the world. Making these drawings gave her a yen to travel again. Ham call: K6ADT

Photo by Neal Swanberg

www.ingramcontent.com/pod-product-compliance
Lightning Source LLC
Chambersburg PA
CBHW071223130626
46555CB00004B/1821